I0813278

BLASTOFF! READERS, AN IMPRINT OF BELLWETHER MEDIA BY FLUTTERBEE

Blastoff! Readers are carefully developed by literacy experts to build reading stamina and move students toward fluency by combining standards-based content with developmentally appropriate text.

Level 1 provides the most support through repetition of high-frequency words, light text, predictable sentence patterns, and strong visual support.

Level 2 offers early readers a bit more challenge through varied sentences, increased text load, and text-supportive special features.

Level 3 advances early-fluent readers toward fluency through increased text load, less reliance on photos, advancing concepts, longer sentences, and more complex special features.

★ **Blastoff! Universe**

Reading Level

Grade K

Grades 1–3

Grade 4

This edition first published in 2026 by Bellwether Media, Inc.

For information regarding permission, write to Bellwether Media, Inc., Attention: Permissions Department, 3500 American Blvd W, Suite 150, Bloomington, MN 55431.

Library of Congress Cataloging-in-Publication Data is available at www.loc.gov or upon request from the publisher.

ISBN: 9798893047776 (hardcover)
ISBN: 9798893048773 (ebook)

Editor: Suzane Nguyen   Designer: Andrea Schneider

Printed in the United States of America, North Mankato, MN.

Table of Contents

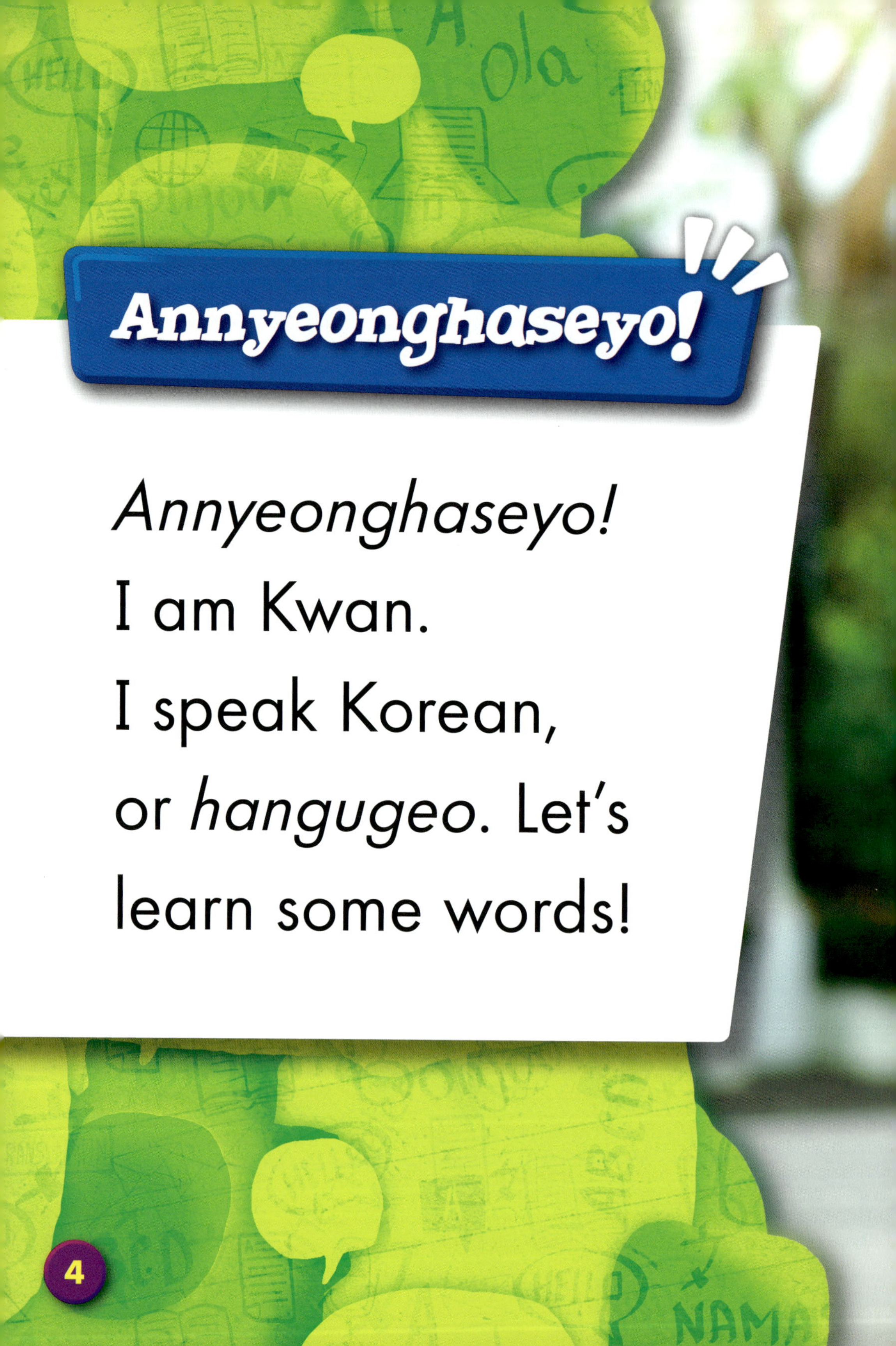

Annyeonghaseyo!

Annyeonghaseyo! I am Kwan. I speak Korean, or *hangugeo*. Let's learn some words!

annyeonghaseyo
(ahn-nyong-hah-say-yoh)
hello
Words to Know
• 네 = yes
ne (neh)
• 아니요 = no
aniyo (ah-nee-yoh)
• 한국어 = Korean
hangugeo (hahn-goo-goh)
• 감사합니다 = thank you
gamsahamnida
(gahm-sah-hahm-nee-dah)

Korean is spoken in North Korea and South Korea. Korean is written in **Hangul**.

Korean-speaking Countries
North Korea
South Korea

At Home

Ji-woo lives with her *gajok*.
Here is their *jip*.

eomma
appa
jip
gajok
Words to Know
•집 = house
jip (cheep)
•가족 = family
gajok (kah-jok)
•아빠 = dad
appa (ah-pah)
•엄마 = mom
eomma (oh-mah)

It is early in the *achim*. Gun-woo eats **kimchi** and *bap* for breakfast.

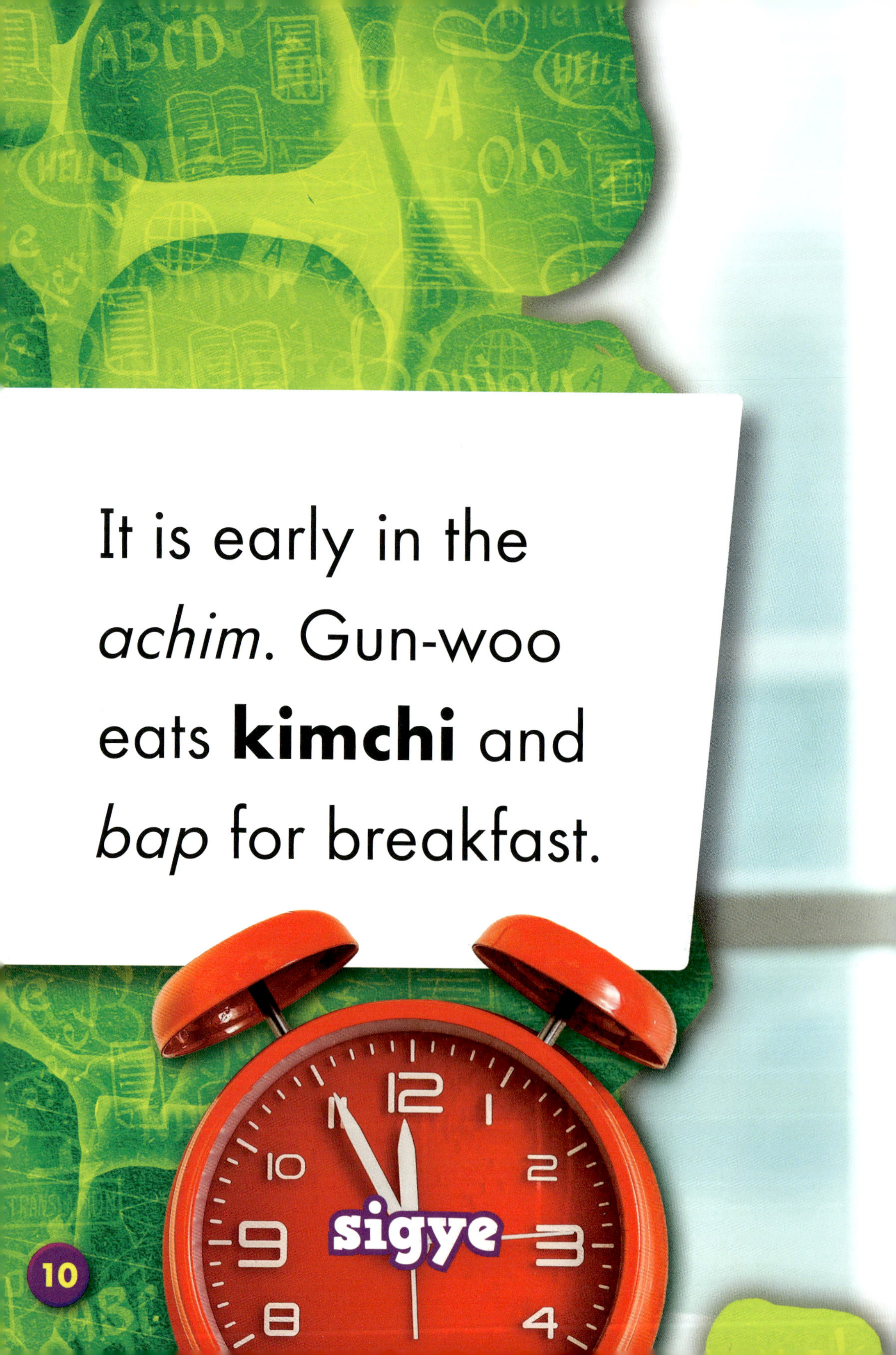

Words to Know
•아침 = morning
achim (ah-cheem)
•밥 = rice
bap (pahp)
•식탁 = dining table
siktak (sheek-tahk)
•시계 = clock
sigye (shee-gay)
bap

At School

Chun-hee walks to *hakgyo*. She says hello to the *seonsaengnim*.

Words to Know
• 학교 = school
hakgyo (hahk-kyoh)
• 선생님 = teacher
seonsaengnim (son-sang-neem)
• 반친구 = classmate
ban chingu (pahn cheen-goo)
• 배낭 = backpack
baenang (pay-nahng)
seonsaengnim
ban chingu

Ji-ho sits at his *chaegsang*. He likes *suhak* class.

Count in Korean

하나... hana (hah-nah)....... 1
둘...... dul (tool)......... 2
셋...... set (seht)................ 3
넷...... net (deht)......... 4
다섯... daseot (tah-soht)... 5
여섯... yeoseot (yoh-soht)...... 6
일곱... ilgop (eel-gohp)..... 7
여덟... yeodeol (yoh-dohl)..... 8
아홉... ahop (ah-hop).... 9
열...... yeol (yohl)............... 10

Words to Know

- 책상 = **desk**
  chaegsang (chek-sahng)
- 수학 = **math**
  suhak (soo-hahg)
- 연필 = **pencil**
  yeonpil (yon-peel)
- 교과서 = **textbook**
  gyogwaseo (kyo-gwah-so)

For Fun

Sook and her *chingu* play together. She is the best at *chukgu*!

Words to Know

- 친구 = **friend(s)**
  chingu (cheen-goo)
- 축구 = **soccer**
  chukgu (chook-goo)
- 농구 = **basketball**
  nonggu (nong-goo)
- 야구 = **baseball**
  yagu (yah-goo)

Yu-jin listens to *eumak* with *hedeupon*. Her favorite group is BLACKPINK.

Words to Know

- 음악 = **music**
  eumak (oo-mahk)
- 헤드폰 = **headphones**
  hedeupon (heh-deu-pon)
- 노래 = **song**
  norae (noh-ray)
- 가수 = **singer**
  gasu (kah-soo)

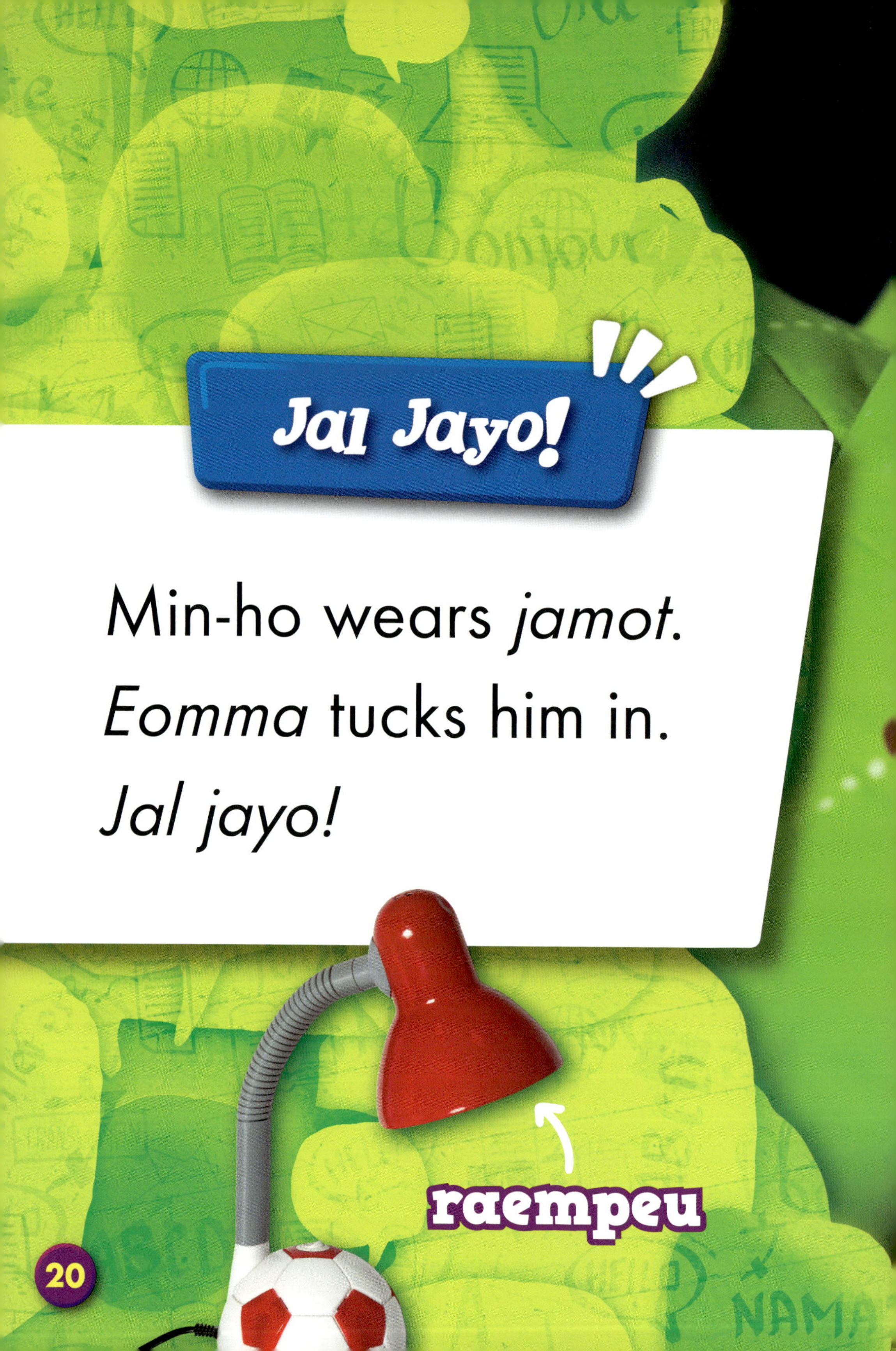

Jal Jayo!

Min-ho wears *jamot*.

Eomma tucks him in.

Jal jayo!

jal jayo
(chal jah-yoh)
good night

i-bul

begae

Words to Know

- 잠옷 = pajamas
jamot (cha-mot)
- 베개 = pillow
begae (pay-gay)
- 램프 = lamp
raempeu (lamp-poo)
- 이불 = blanket
i-bul (ee-pull)

Glossary

Hangul

the alphabet used to write Korean

kimchi

a flavorful Korean dish made of pickled vegetables

To Learn More

AT THE LIBRARY

Langdo, Bryan. *South Korea*. Minneapolis, Minn.: Bellwether Media, 2025.

Nguyen, Suzane. *Blackpink*. Minneapolis, Minn.: Bellwether Media, 2026.

Park, Aerin. *See and Say Korean*. North Mankato, Minn.: Capstone, 2025.

ON THE WEB

FACTSURFER

Factsurfer.com gives you a safe, fun way to find more information.

1. Go to www.factsurfer.com.
2. Enter "Korean" into the search box and click 🔍.
3. Select your book cover to see a list of related content.

Index

The images in this book are reproduced through the courtesy of: eyesfoto, front cover; Aptyp_koK, p. 3; ANURAK PONGPATIMET, pp. 4-5; UN2, p. 6 (Hangul); Image Republic, pp. 6-7; TongRo Images/ Alamy Stock Photo, pp. 8-9; miro, p. 10 (sigye); lalalululala, pp. 10-11; BillionPhotos.com, p. 12 (baenang); paulaphoto, pp. 12-13; Markz | Dreamstime.com, p. 14 (gyogwaseo); Ground Picture, pp. 14-15; MERCURY studio, p. 16 (nonggu); FatCamera, pp. 16-17; Prostock-studio, pp. 18-19; krolya25, p. 20 (raempeu); kdshutterman, pp. 20-21; jang jongseok, p. 22 (Hangul); Nunung Noor Aisyah, p. 22 (kimchi).